# ANIMAL LIVES

*The Frog*

KINGFISHER
Kingfisher Publications Plc
New Penderel House, 283–288 High Holborn,
London WC1V 7HZ

First published by Kingfisher Publications Plc 2000
2 4 6 8 10 9 7 5 3 1

1TR/1199/SC/RPR(RPR)/150NYM

A CIP catalogue record for this book is available
from the British Library.

ISBN 0 7534 0363 3

Series editor: Miranda Smith
Series designer: Sarah Goodwin

Printed in Hong Kong

# ANIMAL LIVES
## *The Frog*

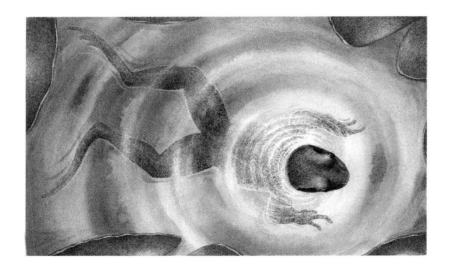

Illustrated by
Bert Kitchen

Written by
Sally Tagholm

KINGFISHER

The bright spring sun creeps gently through the undergrowth, drying the tiny drops of rain on the ferns and bracken. It is time to wake up after the long quiet winter months. The smooth speckled frog slips quietly out of the darkness into the soft warm air. He sits, eyes blinking in the brightness. As usual, he has hibernated under the same small rock at the bottom of the ditch — a safe, secret hiding-place.

He is hungry after his long sleep, but waits patiently, perfectly camouflaged against the green shoots and old brown leaves. It is not long before he spots his first meal – a juicy pink worm slithering slowly through the soft earth. He bides his time, toes twitching. Then he pounces, seizing the wriggling prey in his gaping mouth. He scrapes off the dirt with delicate fingers before gulping it down whole.

He leaps off silently through the long damp grass, heading for the cool, fresh water of the pond which is his summer home. There will be plenty more food on the way – slugs, caterpillars and, perhaps, the odd spider. His strong back legs arch and stretch as they push him high in the air, then fold beneath him as he lands, neatly hinged. A small black fly drowsing in the sun stops him short in his tracks and his long sticky tongue darts out in a flash, scooping the insect greedily into his mouth.

I t is not far to the pond where the wild iris blooms and the shady lilypads float on the dark surface like small green flying saucers. But he must be very careful. There are all kinds of hungry creatures lurking. Suddenly, he is surprised by the large hedgehog who nests in the leaves under the hollow oak tree. She chases him at an alarming speed, shuffling along on her short, stout legs, spines quivering. He manages to give her the slip, launching himself through the air with his most athletic leaps until, at last, he plunges into the safety of the water.

He surfaces again, briefly, curving upwards through the duckweed with a plop, to snatch a gulp of air before diving down through the murky water. His strong hind legs slice smoothly behind him, their large webbed feet splayed out like slippery paddles. But soon he turns and heads back up towards the sunshine. He clambers onto a lilypad and joins the choir of male frogs each croaking to find a mate. It is a tuneless din, which saws through the air like a rusty orchestra.

The pouch in his throat blows up like a tiny balloon, turning the air he breathes out of his lungs into an impressively loud croak. He doesn't even have to open his mouth or move his lips so he can perform just as efficiently underwater if he wants to. Before long, a female responds, grunting quietly in reply. She hops slowly down the steep bank, rustling through the meadowsweet and reeds. Her smooth, damp chest is red just now, and her body is fat and bulging with eggs. Each year, like clockwork, she comes back to the pond when it is the breeding season. She moves slowly after her journey and slithers carefully into the cool water to join her new mate. All around them, the croaky chorus continues, filling the peaceful air.

They set off, synchronized swimmers in the same brown camouflage. He climbs on board piggyback, clasping her firmly under her arms so his fingers meet across her chest. He has a special spiny patch on each thumb which helps him get a good grip. They swim like this in their shadowy embrace for one whole day and one whole night before she releases her stream of microscopic eggs. The male fertilizes them with his sperm before they sink to the bottom of the pond and the frogs part.

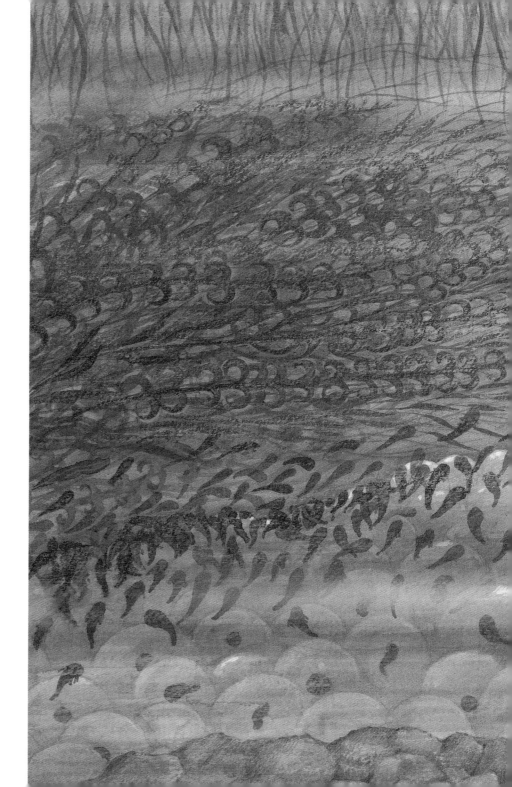

The tiny black eggs have no shells of their own but are protected by a layer of jelly. This swells in the water, glueing the eggs together and floating up to the surface. The sun gently warms the frogspawn as the tadpoles grow, neatly curled inside their capsules, tempting food for ducks and fish. After two weeks, the tadpoles who have survived will hatch and wriggle free into the water.

Once they have left their floating nursery, the tiny, newly hatched tadpoles cling tightly to the nearest weeds, swaying this way and that, like extra leaves. After a few days, their mouths and eyes open and they dart off through the water, long tails wriggling, breathing through special feathery gills just behind their heads. They swarm together in a school, eating a soup of slimy, green algae. But a fleet of predators lurks, including newts who have also returned to the pond to breed.

The tadpoles grow rapidly from day to day and, before long, they start to lose their familiar, slippery shape. Miniature back legs sprout, fully jointed and froglike, fitted with tiny webbed feet. Lungs develop inside their small bodies and smooth new skin covers the gills they no longer need. They swim to the surface, odd, in-between creatures no longer tadpoles but not yet frogs, and help themselves to floating insects and grubs. Within a month, their short, front legs will appear, elbows first, turning them into minute froglets with wriggling tails.

It is midsummer now and the thick reeds point their long green fingers high in the blue sky. The tadpoles have turned into perfectly formed miniature frogs, no bigger than a baby's fingernail. It will be another three years before they are fully grown. Their tails have slowly shrunk and vanished and they have shed their old tight tadpole skins. They have already started to hop out of the water and sit like tiny shiny statues on the smooth grey rocks. Soon, they will swarm onto the banks of the pond, ready to investigate the world beyond.

But the froglets are defenceless and few will survive to adulthood. They are at the mercy of many creatures both in the water and on land. They must be especially careful of the big grey herons who stalk through the shadows, stabbing the water with their long, yellow bills. They are feeding young nestlings and need to find plenty of beetles, water voles – and tender young froglets!

The breeding season is over and the adult frogs are quiet now, peering out from their hiding places around the pond. Others, submerged in duckweed, watch with periscope eyes as tiny froglets hop high in the air like miniature gymnasts. Below the surface, tadpoles of all shapes and sizes, some freshly hatched, others almost fully formed, grow to adulthood.

# THE COMMON FROG

**Scientific name:** *Rana temporaria*

**Other names:** Grass frog, brown frog.

**Size:** Adult males are approximately 7.5cms long. Adult females are approximately 8.75cms long.

**Distribution:** Europe and Asia, with close relatives in America and Australia.

**Habitat:** Damp grass, undergrowth, ditches, ponds.

**Food:** Insects, slugs, earthworms, caterpillars, spiders.

**Predators:** Fish (e.g. pike), rats, otters, hedgehogs, badgers, newts, snakes, herons, owls.

**Special characteristics:** Smooth, moist skin which helps to absorb oxygen, strong hind legs with webbed feet, protruding eyes with transparent lids and excellent all-round vision, and a long, sticky tongue.

**Call:** Each species of frog has a unique call so that only members of the same species will react to it. It is produced by the male frog filling his lungs with air, then closing his mouth and nostrils. The air is moved backwards and forwards from the lungs to the inflated vocal pouch over the vocal chords. This creates a croaking sound.

# ABOUT THE FROG

The common frog is found in Europe and the cooler parts of Asia but it has close relatives scattered all over the world. These include flying frogs that can glide through the rainforest, and spadefoot frogs that burrow underground. The largest frog in the world is the Goliath frog of West Africa that can grow to more than 300mm in length. One of the smallest frogs lives in Brazil in South America and is only 9.8mm long.

## AFRICAN REED FROG

These African frogs have an especially loud croak that can be heard several kilometres away. They need to make a loud noise to attract a mate because they live in tall reeds and are difficult to see.

## TREE FROG

Tree frogs are usually smaller than frogs that live on the ground so that they can climb more easily. They have small suckers on their long toes to help them get a good grip. Tree frogs live in warm countries like Australia.

## SOUTH AMERICAN ARROW POISON FROG

Unlike most other frogs, these do not escape from danger by hiding or leaping away. Instead they use their brilliantly coloured markings to show that they are dangerous to eat. Their skin is so poisonous that some South American Indians use the poison for their blow darts.

# FROG WORDS

**algae** microscopic water plants that look like green slime

**amphibian** creature that lives both on land and in the water

**breeding season** time of year when mating occurs

**froglet** tiny, fully formed frog

**frogspawn** mass of frogs' eggs enclosed in jelly

**gills** external organs through which tadpoles breathe by taking oxygen from the water they live in

**hibernate** to sleep through the winter

**predator** creature that hunts and kills for food

**prey** creature that is hunted for food

**tadpole** tiny, long-tailed hatchling from a frog's egg that lives underwater

**webbed feet** feet with toes joined together by skin

# USEFUL CONTACTS

**Froglife**
Triton House, Bramfield,
Halesworth, Suffolk IP19 9AE
Tel: 01986 784518

**The Wildlife Trusts**
The Kiln, Waterside, Mather Road,
Newark NG24 1WT
Tel: 01636 670000

**World Wide Fund for Nature**
Panda House, Weyside Park,
Godalming, Surrey GU7 1XR
Tel: 01483 426444

**The Herpetological Conservation Trust**
655A Christchurch Road, Boscombe,
Bournemouth, Dorset BH1 4AP
Tel: 01202 391319

**Young Herpetologists' Club**
British Herpetological Society,
c/o The Zoological Society of London,
Regent's Park, London NW1 4RY
Tel: 020 8452 9578

# INDEX

# ACKNOWLEDGEMENTS

*The author and publishers thank Muriel Kitchen and John Tagholm for the photographs on the jacket.*